Hold on to your hat and grab your magnifying glass— the Great Bible Adventure is about to begin! As you read each story, you'll see that the Bible is full of surprises: Bad guys become good guys, people get swallowed by whales, and a little kid with a slingshot wins a fight against a giant!

Each exciting story has special pictures hidden in the illustration, so you can play detective while you discover some of the amazing people and events in the Bible. Whether you're an amateur sleuth or a seasoned pro at uncovering buried treasure, you'll continue to find new surprises every time you read the stories.

Let the Adventure Begin!

The Great Bible Adventure

S A N D Y S I L V E R T H O R N E

HARVEST HOUSE PUBLISHERS
Eugene, Oregon 97402

More "Finders" For Seekers...

 Walking shark

 Flying kite

 Welcome mat

 Dog fish

 Man taking a bath

 Dog soldier

 Beggar

 Lady with a big waterpot

 Ancient Egyptian

 Nebuchadnezzar's mailboxes

 Cow in a man mask

 Goliath's tent

 Someone dropping a cake

 A crowded roof

 The potter

 Kid with a slingshot

 Electric eel

 Worried resident

 Man carrying his cow

 Swimmer

 Horse cooling off

 Tax collector's table

 Archery target

Man carrying a load

 Guy with a map

 Catfish

 Two sheep dressed like a citizen of Jerusalem

 Kid with a huge fish

 Balancing act

 Cue card

 Very long straw

 sail fish

 Babylonian dressing room

 Doubtful citizen

 Philistine poster

 Babylonian citizen

 Three bandits

 Juggler

 Two traveling salesmen

 Sunbather

 Boy and his dog

 Fish kabob

 Zaccheus' ten money bags

 Twenty-two full sacks of Joseph's grain

 Ten prodigal bucks

Ask and it will be given to you;
seek and you will find;
knock and the door will be opened to you.
For everyone who asks receives;
he who seeks finds; and to him who knocks,
the door will be opened.

—Matthew 7:7,8

NOAH

Noah refused to listen to the taunts and jeers of his neighbors. "Hey, turkey!" they called. "Why are you building a boat on dry land?" At times, Noah must have wondered if he really *was* crazy. But God had told him to build an ark and he wasn't going to disobey the voice of the Lord.

At last the huge boat was finished, and Noah, his wife and sons began the enormous task of filling it with grain and water. Then the animals started to arrive. Elephants, lions, horses and more filed into the hull by twos without so much as a scuffle between them. (Look for 24 pairs.) As the first raindrops began to fall, God sealed the door shut. Noah's family and all the animals were safe inside.

For 40 days and 40 nights the rain fell from cloud-blackened skies. Before long, the earth was covered with water. At the end of 40 days, Noah opened a tiny window at the top of the ark. Blue sky! What a wonderful sight after so many days of darkness. After waiting for the waters to go down, Noah released a dove and watched until it disappeared. "Fly away!" he called after it, "and bring me back a sign!"

In the evening, the dove returned with an olive branch in it's mouth, indicating that the long days of waiting were almost over. How thankful Noah and his family were to feel dry land beneath their feet once again! As they praised God, a beautiful rainbow appeared to remind them that God always keeps His promises and that He would never again cause a flood to cover the whole earth.

JOSEPH

Joseph looked up from the pit to see his eleven brothers sneering down at him. He heard them barter with the leader of a passing caravan and before long he was pulled out of the pit and sold into slavery for 20 pieces of silver.

In Egypt, he was bought by a man named Potipher. Joseph was talented and would have done well, were it not for Potipher's wife. She became angry with the young Hebrew and lied about him to her husband. In a rage, Potipher had Joseph thrown into prison, as if he didn't have enough troubles already!

But Joseph still trusted God, and because he did, God rewarded him.

One night Pharaoh, the king of Egypt, had a strange dream. The vision of cows and grain disturbed him so much that when he awoke he called all the wise men of Egypt together to interpret it. No one except his cupbearer could offer the king any help. "Send for Joseph," the cupbearer said. "He will tell you what it means."

After more than two years in prison, Joseph suddenly found himself standing before Pharaoh. "God will give you the meaning of your dream," Joseph told him. "You must begin storing up food now, because a great famine is coming."

Pharaoh was so impressed by Joseph's answer that he put him in charge of gathering and storing the food. Because of the famine, Joseph's brothers, along with thousands of other people, traveled to Egypt to buy grain. Although Joseph could have destroyed his sinful brothers in revenge, he chose to forgive them instead. Because he loved his family, he was able to help them.

MOSES

Moses felt he had nowhere to turn. Before him lay the Red Sea and behind him, the armies of Egypt were in hot pursuit, led by an angry Pharaoh . Had Moses rescued his brother Aaron, his sister Miriam, and all the Israelites from slavery only to have them die like this? He could feel the panic growing among the people. "Better to have stayed in Egypt than to die in the wilderness!" they yelled at him.

Moses and his two generals, Joshua and Caleb, knew there was nothing to do except trust God. "Stretch out your hand over the sea, Moses, and I will save you," the Lord told him.

All the people watched as Moses lifted his hand. Suddenly, a fierce wind cut into the sea like a knife, dividing it before their eyes. Two towering, wet walls rose up on either side, as Moses led God's children through to safety.

Pharaoh would have been smart to give up the chase. But his head was filled with hatred and greed. And what of the valuable treasure  given to the Israelites at their departure? His slaves *must* not escape! Spurring their horses on, the armies of Egypt raced between the liquid walls. As suddenly as it had started, the wind stopped. Tons of water crashed down upon their heads, engulfing Pharaoh and his army.

JOSHUA

Joshua's voice rang with authority. "God wants you to march around the city for seven days," he told the people. "On the seventh day the trumpets will sound and you must all shout with a loud voice. Then the walls of Jericho will fall!"

The Israelites looked at the massive fortress before them. By shouting and playing trumpets, they would conquer Jericho? Perhaps the hot sun and responsibilities of leadership had sent Joshua over the edge! Nevertheless, he was their leader and they would obey him. After all, stranger things than this had happened on their journey toward the Promised Land.

Obediently, they began to march, carrying the Ark of the Covenant Imagine how the people of Jericho must have laughed at the ridiculous sight as they looked down from their safe, high towers. But their laughter quickly turned to tears when, on the seventh day, the trumpets played and the shouts of the Israelites filled the air. The walls crumbled before them and God's children conquered the city. The king of Jericho and all his people were destroyed—all except one woman named Rahab . She and her family were spared because she had trusted in God and had bravely helped the Israelites. By tying a scarlet cord outside her window she was saved.

DAVID

could not believe his eyes or his ears. Down in the valley of Elah stood the ugliest, most enormous giant he had ever seen. Goliath, the famed warrior of the Philistines , was yelling out a challenge. "Come and fight, you pack of cowards!" he bellowed. Fear gripped the army of Israel, and no one answered.

David's older brothers eyed him impatiently. "This is no place for a child," they told him. "Go back home to your sheep !"

David, who had been chosen by the prophet Samuel to be Israel's next king, had no intention of leaving. "I will fight the Philistine," he said boldly. "God has delivered me from a lion and a bear , and he will deliver me from Goliath!"

King Saul  was not convinced. But since *he* had no intention of fighting the giant, he gave David his armor and said, "God be with you." The young boy felt like a snail in a turtle's shell wearing the bulky metal shirt. Jonathan , King Saul's son, helped him remove the heavy armor. Grabbing his sling and five stones from a nearby stream , David was ready to face the enemy.

When Goliath saw David coming toward him, he laughed and cursed. "I'll throw your carcass to the vultures and wolves !" he yelled.

But David answered in a strong voice, "You come to me with a spear and a shield , but I come in the name of the living God!"

Before the giant could even raise his sword, a stone whizzed through the air and hit him smack in the middle of his forehead! Goliath fell to the ground, never to rise again.

FIERY FURNACE

The fiery furnace blazed with white heat  Flames shot higher and higher as King Nebuchadnezzar cried, "Seven times hotter than usual!" His face purple with rage, the king looked as if he might explode into flames himself!

Shadrach, Meshach, and Abednego were about to be thrown into the heart of the fire because they refused to bow down to a golden image of the king whenever the horns , flutes , and lyres were played. Trusting in the living God, they knew it was a sin to worship idols.

Nebuchadnezzar chose the mightiest warriors in the army to bind the three men and hurl them into the flames. The blast of heat from the furnace killed the warriors instantly. Eagerly, the king waited for Shadrach, Meshach, and Abednego to disintegrate. But it never happened.

The king's eyes almost popped out of his head in shock. Was he crazy, or did he see *four* men standing unharmed in the killing heat? The fourth figure looked like the Son of God.

Inching closer to the mouth of the furnace, he called for Shadrach Meshach, and Abednego to come out. All the princes , governors counselors , and captains trembled in awe when the three men walked toward them. Not a hair on their heads had been singed, and not a corner of their coats had turned black. They didn't even smell like smoke! Because they were faithful, God spared their lives.

JONAH

"Jonah!" the voice of the Lord spoke to His prophet. "Go to the city of Nineveh  and preach against their wickedness."

The thought of facing that evil, bloodthirsty bunch scared Jonah so badly that he disobeyed God. Instead, he packed up his ten sermon notes , along with his six pieces of luggage, and headed out of town. Boarding a ship he sailed as far away from Nineveh as possible.

"I'm safe," Jonah thought, looking out on the calm sea, "God will never find me here."

It wasn't long before disaster struck. The sky turned dark and a fierce wind whipped the waters into huge, angry waves

The sailors were terrified that the ship would sink. "It's my fault!" Jonah confessed, yelling above the roar of the storm. "Throw me overboard and you'll be saved!" Reluctantly, the sailers tossed him into the raging sea.

Jonah was sure he was lost, but God sent a giant fish to swallow him and take him back to shore. After three days the fish threw Jonah up on land and there he lay, a wet, frightened, lump of misery.

You can imagine how well Jonah learned his lesson. He probably set a world record racing back to Nineveh! The prophet preached with such conviction that the whole city repented and turned to God.

MARY and JOSEPH

Mary and Joseph arrived late at night in  Bethlehem, only to find the town over-flowing with travelers. Just like them, everyone had obeyed the orders of the Roman soldiers to return to their birthplace to be counted by a census-taker.

Carefully, Joseph helped his wife down from the donkey. How would they ever find a place to stay? Mary was ready to give birth to her first child and needed rest. Banging on the door of an inn, Joseph prayed they would have room. "No!" the innkeeper said shortly. Then he looked past Joseph and saw Mary. His heart softened. "Well, I suppose you could stay in the stable. It's not much, but it's warm and dry."

That night something happened that changed the world forever. In the lowly stable far from the palace of a king, God's Son was born. Mary wrapped her baby Jesus in clean cloths and lay him in a manger. There was no gilded cradle and no soft pillow for the King above all kings.

On that wondrous night, shepherds in the fields looked up at the moonlit sky. Suddenly an angel appeared and told them of Jesus' birth. Praising God, they hurried to worship the child.

Later, wise men came searching for Jesus. They had seen His bright star in the east and had hurried to bow before the King of kings and offer him precious gifts. Christ Jesus, the Lord, had been born!

JESUS

Jesus and his mother  were talking to the servants. Inside the other room, wedding guests sang and danced and enjoyed the celebration. Mary had noticed that the casks of wine were empty, and soon the wedding guests' glasses would be empty, too. "Do whatever my Son says," Mary told the servants. "And please don't tell the bride and groom about the wine. We don't want to worry them."

The servants looked at Jesus expectantly. What would He ask of them? "Fill those six water-pots with water," said Jesus, pointing to the huge stone pots. "Then pour some into a goblet and take it to the headwaiter."

The servants followed His orders, though it must have seemed ridiculous to them. Expecting the headwaiter to be angry, they waited anxiously as he raised the glass to his mouth. He took a gulp and smacked his lips with pleasure. "Well, this certainly is a surprise!" he told them. "Most people serve the best wine first and save the worst for later. But you have saved the best wine for last!"

The servants looked at Jesus in wonder. Who was this Man that could change water into wine? None of the guests, the bride, or the groom realized what Jesus had done. But the servants knew. They witnessed Jesus' first miracle!

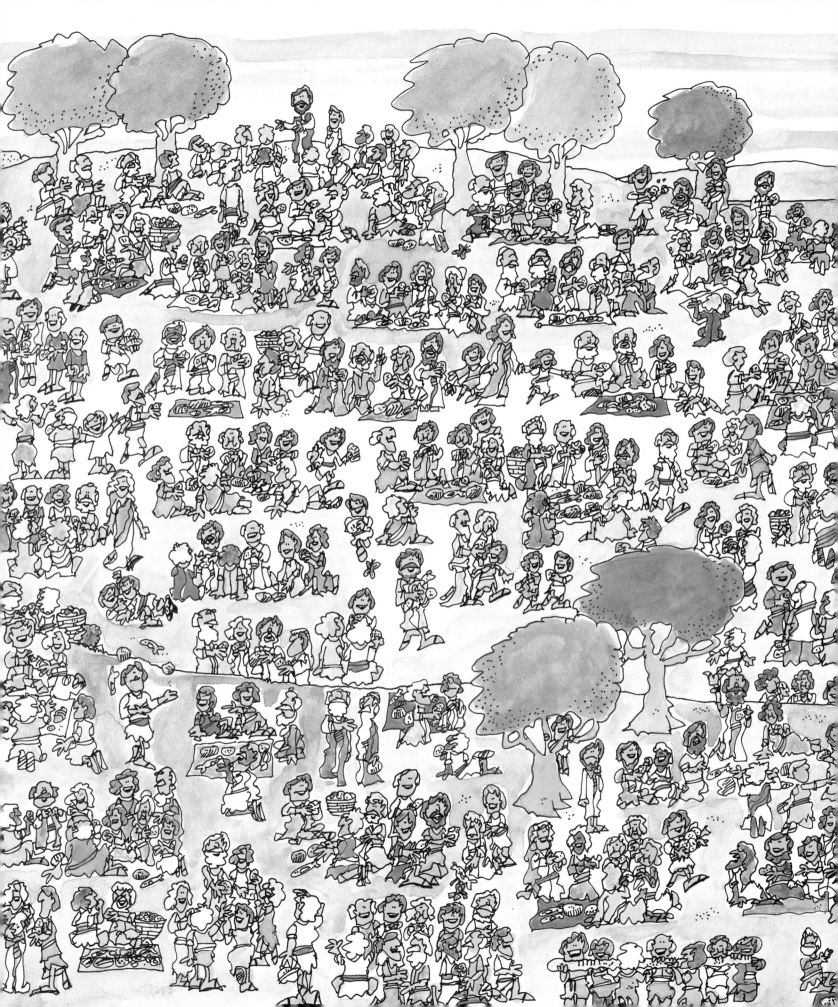

Feeding 5000

Feeding 5000 people, all hungry and far from home, would not be easy. In fact, it would be impossible! "Even if we spent a fortune on bread," said Phillip , "we still wouldn't have enough to satisfy everyone."

Peter's brother Andrew had noticed a little boy with five loaves of bread and two fish . "Perhaps he could share his lunch?" Andrew suggested lamely. "Bad idea," he added quickly, when he saw the other disciples look at him as if he were insane.

But Jesus thought it was a great plan! "Tell the people to sit down on the grass," He said. Then He thanked God for the bread and fish. Handing the food to His disciples, Jesus told them, "Pass it around and make sure that everyone has enough."

Incredibly, that tiny lunch turned into an enormous feast! Five thousand hungry mouths kept gobbling up food, asking for seconds and thirds. When they were all finished, the disciples collected what remained. The leftover bread and fish filled twelve baskets !

Everyone was so amazed by this miracle that they wanted Jesus to become their king—even if it meant taking Him by force! They didn't understand who He was, or why He had come into the world.

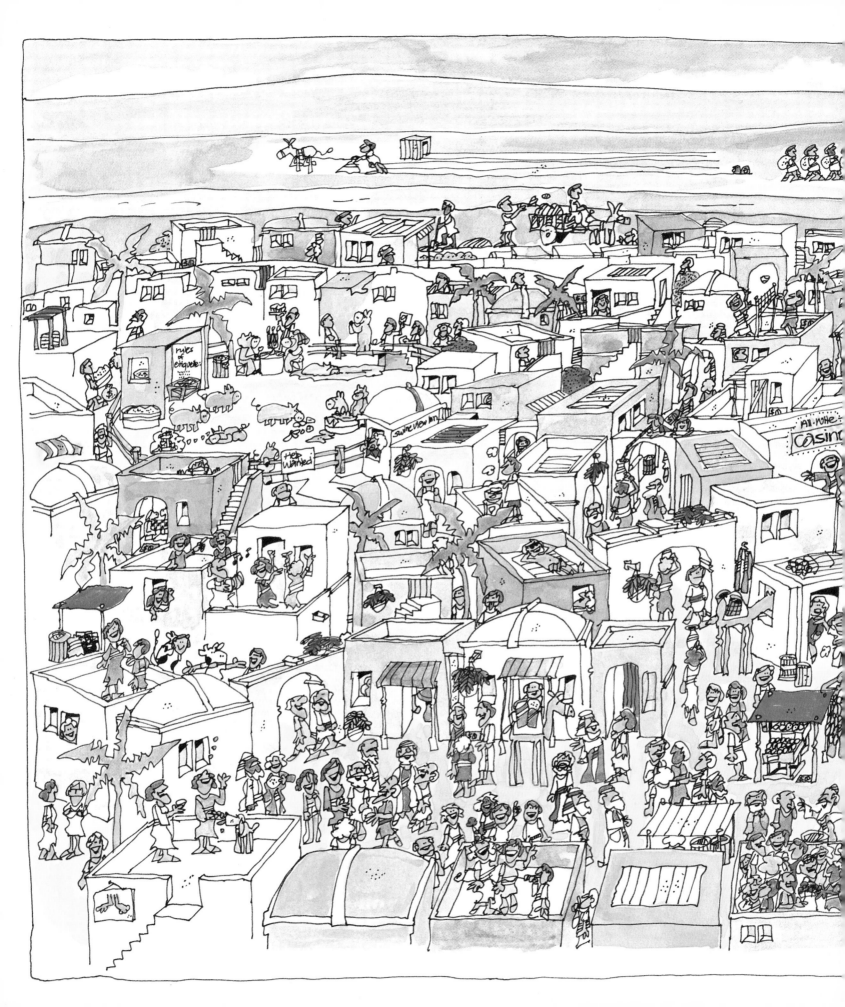

The PRODIGAL SON

The prodigal son was surrounded by fat, greasy, smelly pigs. His clothes were in rags and his bare feet were ankle-deep in muck and slime. "I'll die of hunger!" he thought in despair. Perhaps if he returned home, his father would let him work as a hired hand. "Why, oh why, did I ever leave?"

Only a few short months ago he had asked his father for his inheritance. Taking the money, he had run away and wildly spent every penny. Alone and deserted by his friends, the only job he could find was in a pig sty.

Tired and almost dead with hunger, the young man headed for home. "I'll ask my father to forgive me," he thought as he drew near the house. But he knew there was little hope.

Imagine his amazement when, looking up, he saw his father running to greet him. "My son, my son!" he cried, hugging and kissing him.

In a daze, the young man was led inside the house. A fine robe was placed around his shoulders and he was given a ring to wear. When the eldest son saw what his father had done, he became jealous and angry. "How dare his disobedient brother be accepted back so easily!"

But nothing could spoil the father's joy. "Let the banquet begin!" he cried happily. "My son was lost, but now he has come home."

ZACCHEUS

Zaccheus was a sly little tax collector. Not only was he selfish, greedy, and rich, but he was dishonest and cheated people when collecting their money. No wonder he wasn't popular!

One day Zaccheus heard that Jesus was coming to Jericho. Hurrying as fast as his short legs could carry him, he ran to find the wonderful teacher. But Jesus was already surrounded by a crowd. Poor Zaccheus was so short that he couldn't see over the tops of their heads, even though he stood on tiptoe and jumped up and down.

But Zaccheus wasn't about to give up. He ran ahead of the crowd and scurried up a sycamore tree. At last he could see, but he never dreamed that Jesus would notice *him*!

"Zaccheus, come down!" called Jesus. "And hurry—I'm staying at your house today."

Zaccheus slid to the ground, amazed at his good fortune. Everyone was shocked, especially the Pharisees. They couldn't understand why Jesus would spend time with such a bad person.

Zaccheus prepared an enormous feast for Jesus, Peter, James, and John. He also invited other tax collectors and outcasts to join them. At the end of the dinner, Zaccheus stood up to make a speech. "Quiet everyone!" he said. "I've decided to give half of my goods to the poor. And if I've cheated anyone, I promise to pay them back four times as much as I took!"

Nothing could have pleased Jesus more. He had come to heal the wounded and to save lost people just like Zaccheus.

"HOSANNA!"

"Hosanna, hosanna!" The joyful shout rang through the streets of Jerusalem. "Blessed is the King who comes in the name of the Lord!" As Jesus rode through the gate, people pressed in on Him from every side, throwing their coats and palm branches on the ground as a carpet for Him.

Oppressed for so long by Roman invaders, the Israelites believed Jesus would become their King and Deliverer. Even Peter, James, John, and the other disciples were filled with thoughts of power and success. No one seemed to notice how humble and sad Jesus was, or that He rode on a donkey instead of a fine, prancing steed. Although the crowds praised their Lord on this day, Jesus knew that soon they would despise and kill Him.

The Pharisees hated Jesus more than anyone and tried to make the people be quiet. But Jesus said, "If they don't praise Me, even the stones will start to shout!"

Jesus arrived at the temple to find it filled with people selling goods. No one had ever seen Him so angry. He smashed their wares and threw the people out.

On that special Palm Sunday morning, Jesus was hailed as King. But it wasn't long before Judas would betray Him, and Jesus would be nailed to a cross in place of the wicked murderer Barabbas. There, He would die in agony for the sins of the world.

"HE IS RISEN!"

"He is risen!" said the angel to Mary  as she stood weeping outside the tomb. Blinking away her tears, the poor woman tried to understand what was happening. Her Lord was not dead, but alive! How could that be?

Only three days ago, Mary and Mary Magdalene had watched as Jesus was taken, bound and bleeding, before Pilate and King Herod . Soldiers spit on Him and beat Him mercilessly. A crown of thorns was placed on His head as He was led out to be crucified. When He died, the sky turned black and the earth shook.

Joseph of Arimathea , a wealthy follower of Jesus, took Jesus' body and laid it in his own tomb. But now the stone was rolled away, and the body was gone! Mary and Mary Magdalene ran to tell Peter , John , and the other disciples.

Although they had lived with Jesus for three years, the disciples never really understood why He had come. Now, at long last, they saw the truth. Could it be that this humble man, who had eaten with sinners such as Zaccheus ; who had fed five thousand people with five loaves of bread and two fish; who had healed the blind; and who had died in Barabbas' place, was, in fact, the Son of God? How the disciples praised their Lord that first Easter morning!

Their praises continued until the time came for Jesus to say good-bye. In wonder, they watched as He blessed them and ascended to heaven. The Son of God had fulfilled His mission. Through His birth, death, and resurrection, Jesus brought salvation to a lost world.

*" **Y**ou will seek me and find me*
when you seek me with all your heart,"
declares the Lord.

—Jeremiah 29:13

Copyright © 1990 by Harvest House Publishers
Eugene, Oregon 97402

Library of Congress Cataloging-in-Publication Data

Silverthorne, Sandy, 1951-
The great Bible adventure: the seek and you will find /
Sandy Silverthorne.
ISBN 0-89081-842-8
1. Bible stories, English.   I. Title.
BS551.2.S54   1990
220.9'505—dc20   90-36385
CIP
AC

Printed in the United States of America.